Winefulness

It's time to stop
and smell the rosé

Introduction

Sometimes, life is hard. Sometimes it's unfair.
Sometimes it knocks you down.

But that's okay. You just need to find yourself a coping
mechanism. A little something that picks you up,
dusts you down, sets you back on your feet and tells
you, "you've got this".

For some, that little something is exercise. A regular
routine of workouts, up at the crack of dawn to stretch
and flex, to push and strain and reach for a final goal,
then bask in the warm, fuzzy glow of endorphins.

For others, it's meditation. Mindfulness. An awareness
of the here and now, and your place in the infinite
cosmos. A chance to take some space to breathe, to
find yourself and clear a moment to be thankful for all
that you are, and all that you have achieved each day.

For us normal people, it's wine.

Because you can rely on wine, can't you? It's there for you when the weight of the world makes itself felt that little bit too much. It's been there for you before, and it'll be there for you again. So it's time to embrace the healing power of wine, to revel in its ability to make even the worst of things that little bit better.

In the coming pages you will find reminders of wine's importance in helping you to find that special calm that allows you to navigate life's occasionally stormy seas. So take a deep breath, pour yourself a glass, turn the page and step out into the still waters of winefulness.

Always remember
the value of fizzical
activity.

Take the time to wine down.

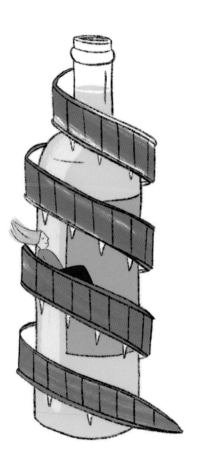

Great minds
drink alike.

You had me
at Merlot.

View the
world through
rosé-tinted
glasses.

Stop and smell
the rosé.

Do things for the right Rieslings.

Learn when to say "yes" and when to say "Pinot".

Believe in the power of fate – after all, que Syrah, Syrah.

Don't take things
at face value
– read between
the wines.

It isn't good
to keep things
bottled up.

Money can't buy
you happiness.
It can, however,
buy you wine.

Never regret
pour decisions.

Sometimes, brut force is the only thing that will work.

You can't do it
all on your own.
Learn when you
can, and when
you Chianti.

Turn up the music
and Rioja 'n' roll.

A smile will get you through hard times – just Grenache and bear it.

Keep Cava and
carry on.

Work hard,
Chardonnay hard.

Life is too short
for sour grapes.

Sometimes you have to work to get your reward: no Champagne, no gain.

Believe in yourself
– you are Proseccond
to none.

If you feel
overwhelmed,
start afresh
with a Sauvignon
Blanc slate.

Let yourself shine
– you were born
to sparkle.

Don't sweat the small stuff – sip happens.

Never deny yourself
life's simple
pleasures: say
"yes way, rosé".

Stay optimistic
– keep your glass
half full.

Friends are essential, so stay close to your partner in wine.

A regular exercise regime is very important.

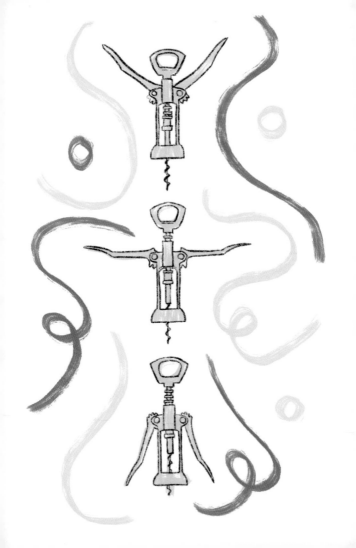

If times are tough,
keep a bucket list
in mind.

On a big birthday,
remember that
age gets better
with wine.

In tough times,
unleash your inner
wine-o-saur.

Keep dreaming of a
white Christmas.
But if it runs out,
drink the red instead.

It's better to
drink outside
the box.

A chat is always
best paired with a
Châteauneuf-du-Pape.

Life is a Cabernet,
after all.

You can't ride the
highs without
experiencing
the Merlots.

Every cloud has a
Syrah lining.

Live, laugh,
Lambrusco.

Practise positive
reinforcement.
Pinot? More like
Pi-hell-yeah!

If you're feeling Merlot, remember tomorrow is another Muscadet.

Keep your feet on the ground – don't get Zinfandelusions of grandeur.

Take some time to dress up nicely. It's good to feel Soave and so-fizz-sticated.

Bored with the daily routine? Add a little Shiraz-matazz to your day.

Sometimes you need to take a gamble in life. Still not enough? Up the Chianti!

But remember,
you cannot
survive on wine
alone. You'll also
need a glass.

Live every moment.
Laugh every day.
Love beyond words.
Limit your alcohol intake.

Please drink responsibly. This book is intended for adults only.

*Thanks go to winefulness experts
Emily Brickell, Natalie Bradley,
Trevor Davies, George Brooker and
Sarah Kyle for their contributions.*

An Hachette UK Company
www.hachette.co.uk

First published in Great Britain
in 2021 by Mitchell Beazley,
an imprint of Octopus Publishing
Group Ltd
Carmelite House
50 Victoria Embankment
London EC4Y 0DZ
www.octopusbooks.co.uk
www.octopusbooksusa.com

Copyright © Octopus Publishing
Group Ltd 2021

Distributed in the US by
Hachette Book Group
1290 Avenue of the Americas
4th and 5th Floors
New York, NY 10104

Distributed in Canada by
Canadian Manda Group
664 Annette St.
Toronto, Ontario, Canada
M6S 2C8

978-1-78472-709-3

A CIP catalogue record for this
book is available from the British
Library.

Printed and bound in China.

10 9 8 7 6 5 4 3 2 1

Commissioning Editor: Joe Cottington
Art Director: Juliette Norsworthy
Assistant Editor: Sarah Kyle
Illustrations: Ella Mclean
Assistant Production Manager: Allison Gonsalves